Pescatarian
COOKBOOK

*70 Easy Recipes For
Mediterranean Dishes With Fish
And Seafood*

Emma Yang

The trademarks that are used are without any consent, and the publication of the trademark is without permission or backing by the trademark owner. All trademarks and brands within this book are for clarifying purposes only and are owned by the owners themselves, not affiliated with this document.

Contents

CHAPTER 4: HEALTHY FISH AND SEAFOOD SOUP RECIPES

Introduction

Cutting meat from your eating regimen may appear to be an immense change. Adopting a Pescatarian diet is quite easy. The key is to never cause yourself to feel like you are forfeiting something or limiting yourself. A Pescatarian diet avoids red meat, poultry, sheep, and pork. You will find vegetables, grains, natural products, beans, cheddar, eggs, and yogurt in a Pescatarian diet. It puts an accentuation on fish and shellfish as a rich source of protein.

Pescatarian diet leads to healthy eating habits and a lifestyle. How we feed our bodies affects our general prosperity. A plant-based eating regimen based on healthy food sources and a fish-driven eating routine loaded with protein has many advantages because of the collaboration of plants and fish.

A Pescatarian diet is protein-stuffed and rich in omega-3s. It decreases congestive cardiovascular breakdown and coronary illness. Sleek fish, specifically (think sardines, mackerel, or salmon), are stacked in unsaturated fats. It advances sufficient omega-3s. Eating fish and seafood expands your admission of omega-3s, which may offer various advantages—from lessening aggravation in the body to advancing cerebrum wellbeing. Notwithstanding greasy fish, chia seeds, flaxseeds, or pecans are incredible plant-based wellsprings of omega-3s.

An eating regimen wealthy in fish and seafood would help supply this imperative supplement. Fish offers a wellspring of complete protein. The intake of Pescatarian food sources can guarantee ideal protein consumption.

Likewise, in contrast to red meat, it is low in soaked fat and better for your heart and pulse hazard. If you are worried about heart wellbeing or have a background marked by coronary illness in your family, you may profit by going Pescatarian.

People choose a Pescatarian diet to lessen their ecological effects by eating fish and plant-based food varieties. It can diminish effects on water biological systems, territory obliteration, undermined species, and overfishing.

The 'Pescatarian Cookbook' offers you 70 healthy recipes that you can have for your Pescatarian diet. The Pescatarian Cookbook is your go-to reference to make the Pescatarian diet a supportable and fulfilling way of life.

Chapter 1: Healthy Fish and Seafood Breakfast Recipes

In a Pescatarian diet, breakfast foods easily fit in the meal plan. Here are some of the healthy and tasty fish and seafood breakfast recipes that you can easily make at home with any difficulty:

1.1 Smoked Salmon Baked Eggs in Avocado

Preparation Time: 10 minutes

Cooking Time: 15 minutes

Serving: 6

Ingredients:

- 3 avocado
- 6 eggs
- 3 slices smoked salmon
- 1 tbsp. of finely chopped Chives
- 1 pinch cayenne pepper
- Toasted bread, for serving

Instructions:

1. Heat oven to 180⁰C.
2. Cut avocados. Put them onto a baking plate.
3. Add salmon to each, and afterward add the egg yolks. Beat the egg whites.

4. Add cayenne pepper and heat for ten minutes, or until the whites have set. Disperse over the chives and a touch of cayenne. Present with toasted bread.

1.2 Smoked Salmon and Dill Waffles

Preparation Time: 40 minutes

Cooking Time: 40 minutes

Serving: 4

Ingredients:

- For Dill Waffles:
- 1 tbsp. granulated sugar
- 1/2 tbsp. baking powder
- 1/2 tsp. table salt
- 3/4 tsp. black pepper
- 1 egg
- 1/4 cup of melted unsalted butter
- 2 tbsp. milk
- 3/4 cup of seltzer
- 2 tbsp. of fresh dill
- For Poached Eggs:
- 4 large eggs
- 2 tsp. white vinegar
- For Serving:

- 8 slices of smoked salmon
- 1/2 cup of Hollandaise Sauce
- Fresh dill, for garnishing

Instructions:

1. In a bowl, whisk together flour, baking powder, sugar, pepper, and salt.
2. Mix egg yolk, dill, milk, seltzer, and butter.
3. In a bowl, beat the egg.
4. Crease egg whites into the waffle maker just until streaks vanish.
5. Preheat the stove to 200°F.
6. Preheat and add a few drops of oil to your waffle iron.
7. Cook waffles until colored and fresh.
8. Transfer waffles in a layer to a wire rack-lined preparing sheet and spot in the oven to keep warm.
9. Fill a bowl with hot water and cover to keep warm.
10. Fill a ten to twelve-inch width, a straight-sided dish with around two cups of water.
11. Mix in vinegar.
12. Cook the eggs for three to four minutes.
13. Move eggs to the bowl of heated water while you make the hollandaise.
14. Spot two cuts of smoked salmon on top of a warm waffle. Eliminate eggs from the warm water with a spoon.

15.   Add the eggs to salmon.

16.   Add hollandaise sauce.

17.   Add dill, and serve.

1.3 Simple Shrimp Scramble

Preparation Time: 15 minutes

Cooking Time: 10 minutes

Serving: 4

Ingredients:

- 1 onion
- 1/4 cup of green pepper
- 1 minced garlic clove
- 3 tbsp. butter, divided
- 1 package of frozen salad shrimp, cooked
- 8 eggs
- 1/2 tsp. salt
- 1/4 tsp. pepper
- 1 cup of cheddar cheese

Instructions:

1. In a huge skillet, sauté the green pepper, onion, and garlic in one tbsp. of butter. Mix in shrimp. Take out in a bowl and keep warm.

2. In a similar skillet, dissolve the remaining butter over medium heat. Add eggs; cook, and mix until totally set. Mix in the shrimp blend, pepper and salt.

3. Sprinkle with cheddar.

4. Cover and let it set for three to five minutes.

1.4 Bacon Lobster Omelet

Preparation Time: 10 minutes

Cooking Time: 10 minutes

Serving: 1

Ingredients:

- 1/4 cup lobster meat
- 1 1/2 cup sour cream
- 1 tsp. of dijon mustard
- 2 eggs
- 1 tbsp. Of water
- 1 tbsp. green onions
- 1/2 tsp. Of dried tarragon
- 1 tsp. of butter
- Salt and pepper, to taste

Instructions:

1. In a small bowl, add sour cream and mustard.

2. In a medium bowl, combine green onions, one egg, tarragon and pepper and salt.

3. Add butter in a skillet, add egg, and then blend and cook till set.

4. Heat butter in a skillet, add the mixture of egg and cook till set.

5. Add sour cream in egg mixture. Blend it and add the lobster meat.

6. Crease another portion of eggs over the lobster side.

7. Serve while warm.

1.5 Seafood Bake with Crispy Hash Brown Topping

Preparation Time: 20 minutes

Cooking Time: 20 minutes

Serving: 4

Ingredients:

- 1 cup of sour cream
- 1 tbsp. Of cornstarch
- 2 tsp. Of lemon zest
- 1 tbsp. Of Dijon mustard
- Pepper, to taste
- Kosher salt, to taste
- 1 1/2 lb. Of mixed seafood
- 1 package of leaf spinach

- 2 cup of frozen hash browns

Instructions:

1. Heat stove to 425^0 F. In a huge bowl, whisk together the sour cream, mustard, cornstarch, lemon zing, and half tsp. each pepper and salt.

2. Add the fish to the cream blend.

3. Add spinach into the mixture of fish.

4. Split between four shallow, one-cup preparing dishes.

5. Add hash browns and brush with olive oil. Cook for twenty to twenty-five minutes.

6. Serve and enjoy.

1.6 Lobster Breakfast Sandwich

Preparation Time: 5 minutes

Cooking Time: 10 minutes

Serving: 4

Ingredients:

- 4 brioche of sandwich buns
- 1 creamy egg
- 1 tsp. of olive oil
- 18 asparagus spears
- 4 lobster tails
- 1 tsp. of chopped fresh chives

Instructions:

1. Part out arranged velvety fried eggs on brioche sandwich buns.
2. Put asparagus sticks softly in olive oil.
3. Put it on the fried eggs, then top with chilled split lobster tail. Sprinkle chives to taste and serve.

1.7 Shrimp and Spinach Omelette

Preparation Time: 5 minutes

Cooking Time: 5 minutes

Serving: 2

Ingredients:

- 10 shrimp
- 6 large eggs
- 1 sprig parsley
- 4 tomatoes
- 1/4 onion
- 1 handful of spinach
- 1 tbsp. of sriracha salt
- 1/4 tsp. of cayenne

Instructions:

1. Cut onion and grape tomatoes.
2. Add onion and salt in a pan.
3. Simultaneously, place the grape tomatoes to broil a bit.
4. When the onions are cooked, toss in spinach, let it wither.
5. Add shrimp.
6. Cook eggs and cover the dish, so the omelet cooks well.
7. Cook for around six to eight minutes.
8. When a slim film of white is covering the yolks, eggs are prepared.
9. Add parsley over it.
10. Serve and enjoy.

1.8 Brunchy Fish and Waffles

Preparation Time: 10 minutes

Cooking Time: 20 minutes

Serving: 4

Ingredients:

- 1 package of Fish Fillets
- 4 Belgian Waffles
- 4 eggs
- 2 tbsp. Of unsalted butter
- One pinch of pepper and pinch of salt
- 1 cup maple syrup
- 1 tbsp. Of fish sauce
- 1/2 cup of honey
- 1 thinly sliced jalapeño
- 1 inch slice fresh ginger
- 2 tsp. Of orange zest
- 1/4 tsp. Of white pepper

Instructions:

1. In a pan over medium-low heat, add butter, maple syrup, fish sauce, honey, ginger, and orange zest, and cook for ten minutes.

2. Let it cool while preparing both fish and waffles as per instructions on the package.

3. Heat butter in a pan.

4. Add eggs and cook until whites have completely set—season with pepper and salt.

5. For serving, place one toasted waffle on a plate. Top with one egg. Stack two fish filets on top of the egg, inclining toward each other to try not to break the yolk.

6. Sprinkle some Jalapeño Maple syrup, and serve.

1.9 Smoked Salmon Hash

Preparation Time: 10 minutes

Cooking Time: 10 minutes

Serving: 2

Ingredients:

- 2 tbsp. olive oil
- 3 red potatoes
- 1 chopped yellow onion
- 1 bell pepper, green
- Kosher salt and black pepper
- 2 tsp. fresh chives, thinly sliced
- 1 1/2 tsp. Of lemon juice
- 2/3 cup sour cream
- 1/2 tsp. Of Dijon mustard
- One salmon fillet

Instructions:

1. Heat the oil in a nonstick skillet over a medium-high flame. Add the onions, potatoes, chime pepper, pepper, and salt, and cook while regularly mixing, until earthy colored, around ten minutes.

2. Cook until the potatoes are delicate, around fifteen minutes more; season to taste with pepper and salt.

3. In the meantime, put sour cream, one tbsp. chives, half tbsp. lemon juice, mustard, half tsp. of salt, and one-eighth tsp. of pepper.

4. Add salmon and one tbsp. lemon juice and keep cooking until warmed through, around two minutes more.

5. Move the hash to plates. Add the one tbsp. of chives and serve with sour cream.

6. Present it with a poached egg on top.

1.10 Alaska Salmon Frittata

Preparation Time: 20 minutes

Cooking Time: 14

Serving: 8

Ingredients:

- 12 beaten eggs
- 1 tbsp. olive oil
- 1 cup of sliced sweet peppers
- 2 1/2 cups broccoli florets
- 1/2 cup of diced onion
- 1 cup salmon
- 1/2 cup frozen peas
- Ground pepper, to taste
- Salt, to taste

Instructions:

1. Preheat broiler to 375^0F
2. Add the broccoli florets, diced onion, cut small-scale sweet peppers in oil.
3. Season with ocean salt and ground dark pepper.
4. Mix in the frozen peas and smoked salmon.
5. Pour in the beaten eggs. Mix well.

6. Keep cooking the frittata, without blending, over the burner for an extra sixty seconds just until the external edge of the frittata starts to set.

7. Place the hot skillet on the stove; cook for ten to fourteen minutes, just until the eggs are set.

8. Allow the frittata to set for five minutes before cutting. Serve hot or cold.

Chapter 2: Healthy Fish and Seafood Lunch and Dinner

Pescatarian lunch and dinner recipes are full of healthy proteins and flavors. There are many varieties of fish and seafood recipes that can be eaten during lunch and dinner time. Following are given some of these recipes that you can try at home:

2.1 Furikake Salmon Bowls

Preparation Time: 10 minutes

Cooking Time: 20 minutes

Serving: 2

Ingredients:

- For Salmon:
- 1 to 2 tbsp. sesame oil
- 1 Pinch pepper, salt and chili flakes
- 8 to 10 ounces of salmon
- 4 ounces of shiitake mushrooms
- For Sauce:
- 3 tbsp. Of soy sauce
- 3 tbsp. Mirin
- 1 tbsp. Furikake
- 1/2 to 2 cups of cooked rice
- 2 bunches of cabbage
- 1 large avocado
- For toppings:
- Scallions
- Cucumber
- Furikake
- Stew pieces

Instructions:

1. Mix mirin and soy sauce in a small bowl.

2. Heat sesame oil in a huge skillet over medium-high heat. Season with pepper and salt.

3. Add the mushrooms and salmon and cook. Turn the heat off, allowing the skillet to cool somewhat.

4. Add sauce over the salmon and mushrooms.

5. Divide rice between two dishes. Sprinkle it with furikake.

6. Put cabbage, avocado wedges, and some other veggies in the bowl.

7. Top with burned salmon and mushrooms, and sprinkle it with Furikake, spooning the excess sauce over the avocado and cabbage.

8. Serve immediately.

2.2 Pan-Seared Halibut over Lemony Zucchini Noodles

Preparation Time: 30 minutes

Cooking Time: 30 minutes

Serving: 2

Ingredients:

- 8 to 10 ounces halibut
- 1 smashed garlic clove
- 1 to 2 tbsp. olive oil
- Pepper, to taste
- Salt, to taste
- For Noodles:
- 1 tbsp. olive oil
- 1 thinly sliced fat shallot
- 3 chopped garlic cloves
- 12 to 16 ounces of zucchini noodles
- pepper, to taste
- Salt, to taste
- 2 tsp. lemon zest
- ½ cup of chopped Italian parsley
- 1 tbsp. Of lemon juice

Instructions:

1. Preheat oven to 375 F. Add garlic cloves in the tray.

2. Season fish with salt and pepper.

3. Place in the oven for about three to six minutes.

4. In a skillet, heat more oil over medium heat and add shallots and garlic, blending until mellowed and fragrant, around three minutes.

5. Add zucchini noodles and season with pepper and salt. Sauté until noodles mellow, around four minutes.

6. Add lemon zing, new parsley, and a crush of lemon. Add salt and lemon. Split between two dishes and top with the halibut.

7. Top with cherry tomatoes, bean stew chips, and pecorino cheddar.

2.3 Rum-Glazed Shrimp

Preparation Time: 10 minutes

Cooking Time: 35 minutes

Serving: 4

Ingredients:

- 1 1/2 lb. Of peeled shrimp
- 3 tbsp. Of olive oil
- 1/3 cup of chili sauce
- 1/4 cup of soy sauce
- 1/4 cup of Rum
- 2 minced cloves garlic
- 1 lime
- 1/2 tsp. Of red pepper flakes
- 1 thinly sliced green onion, to garnish

Instructions:

1. Add shrimp in a bowl.
2. In a bowl, add olive oil, sweet bean stew sauce, soy sauce, rum, garlic, lime juice, and red pepper drops.
3. Let marinate in the cooler for fifteen to thirty minutes.
4. Add shrimp in the oil and cook on one side for around two minutes.

5. Add green onions and serve.

2.4 Air Fryer Salmon

Preparation Time: 7 minutes

Cooking Time: 12 minutes

Serving: 5

Ingredients:

- 2 wild salmon fillets
- 2 tsps. of tsp. avocado oil
- 2 tsps. of paprika
- Black pepper, to taste
- Salt, to taste
- Lemon wedges

Instructions:

1. Eliminate any bones from salmon and set aside for one hour.
2. Rub each fillet with olive oil and season with paprika, salt and pepper.
3. Put fillets in the air fryer at 390 degrees for seven minutes.
4. When the time is over, check fillets with a fork to ensure they are done.

2.5 Garlicky Shrimp Alfredo Bake

Preparation Time: 20 minutes

Cooking Time: 20 minutes

Serving: 4

Ingredients:

- 12 ounces of penne
- 3 minced cloves garlic
- 1 lb. Of raw shrimp
- 3 tbsp. Of divided butter
- 2 tbsp. Of chopped parsley
- Kosher salt, to taste
- 2 tbsp. of flour
- 1/4 cup of chicken broth
- 3/4 cup of milk
- 1cup of shredded mozzarella
- 1/4 cup of grated Parmesan
- Black pepper, to taste
- 1 cup of chopped tomatoes

Instructions:

1. Preheat the stove to 350°F.
2. In a huge pot of water, prepare penne as per instructions on the package.

3. Add shrimp, garlic, and parsley in the oil and season with salt. Cook until the shrimp is pink.

4. Add two tablespoon butter and flour and cook for about one minute.

5. Put milk and stock in it. Mix in mozzarella and Parmesan, pepper, and with salt.

6. Add tomatoes, cooked penne, and shrimp, and throw until consolidated.

7. Sprinkle with mozzarella and two tbsp. parmesan and heat until melted, five to seven minutes.

8. Sprinkle parsley before serving.

2.6 Oysters Rockefeller

Preparation Time: 15 minutes

Cooking Time: 1 hour

Serving: 2 dozen

Ingredients:

- 1 finely chopped medium onion
- 1/2 cup of cubed butter
- 1 package of fresh spinach
- 1 cup of Romano cheese
- 1 tbsp. lemon juice
- 1/8 tsp. pepper
- 2 pounds of kosher salt
- 3 dozen of fresh oysters

Instructions:

1. In a skillet, sauté onion. Add spinach; cook and mix until withered. Eliminate from the heat; mix in cheddar, lemon juice and pepper.

2. Spread salt into two ungreased heating dishes. Add oysters in the base shell.

3. Add salt in the clamshells.

4. Top each with two teaspoons of spinach.

5. Prepare, uncovered, at 450° F until oysters are fully cooked, six to eight minutes. Serve.

2.7 Bruschetta Salmon

Preparation Time: 10 minutes

Cooking Time: 15 minutes

Serving: 4

Ingredients:

- 4 salmon fillets
- 1 tsp. Of dried oregano
- Kosher salt, to taste
- Black pepper, to taste
- 2 tbsp. Of olive oil
- 3 minced cloves garlic
- 2 minced shallots
- 3 cup of cherry tomatoes
- 1/2 lemon
- 1/4 cup of basil
- Parmesan, to serve
- Balsamic glaze
- Toppings:
- Tomatoes, red onion, avocado, jalapeño peppers, and coriander sprigs

Instructions:

1. Season salmon with oregano, salt and pepper.

2. Add salmon in the heated oil and cook for around six minutes.

3. Flip and cook for six minutes until the salmon is misty. Move to a plate.

4. Add remaining tablespoon olive oil to skillet, mix in garlic and shallots. Cook until garlic is fragrant.

5. Add tomatoes and season with salt and pepper.

6. Add lemon juice.

7. Serve salmon with tomato blend spooned on top. Top with basil and Parmesan, sprinkle with balsamic coating.

2.8 Creamed Spinach Stuffed Salmon

Preparation Time: 10 minutes

Cooking Time: 20 minutes

Serving: 2

Ingredients:

- For Salmon:
- 4 salmon fillets
- Pepper and salt, to season
- 2 tbsp. lemon juice
- 2 tbsp. olive oil
- 1 tbsp. unsalted butter
- For Filling:
- 4 ounces cream cheese
- 4 ounces frozen spinach
- 1/4 cup of parmesan cheese
- 2 tsp. minced garlic
- Pepper and salt, to taste
- For Garlic Butter:
- 1 tbsp. unsalted butter
- 1 tbsp. minced garlic
- 1 tbsp. lemon juice

Instructions:

1. Season the two sides with salt, pepper, one tablespoon olive oil, and lemon juice.

2. In a medium-sized bowl, add the spinach, cream cheddar, parmesan cheddar and garlic.

3. Add pepper and salt.

4. Heat butter and oil in a skillet over medium heat.

5. Add the salmon and fry for around six to seven minutes.

6. Cook the other side for around six to seven minutes.

7. Add the garlic and lemon juice; sauté until garlic is fragrant (around 30 seconds). Present with the salmon.

2.9 Shrimp Alfredo

Preparation Time: 30 minutes

Cooking Time: 10 minutes

Serving: 6

Ingredients:

- 10 ounces of fettuccine pasta
- 5 tbsp. butter
- 1 cup of heavy cream
- 3/4 cup of parmesan cheese
- Pepper, to taste
- Salt, to taste
- 1 pound of shrimp
- 1 tsp. minced garlic
- 2 tbsp. chopped parsley

Instructions:

1. Cook the pasta in salted water.
2. Add four tablespoons butter in a pot over medium-low heat.
3. Add the cream and stew for four to five minutes or until just thickened.
4. Add parmesan cheddar, blending consistently until cheddar has softened.
5. Add pepper and salt.
6. Heat one tablespoon butter in a huge skillet over medium-high heat.

7. Add the shrimp and season with salt and pepper.

8. Cook the shrimp for three to four minutes until shrimps are pink and obscure.

9. Add the garlic to the dish and cook for an extra thirty seconds.

10. Add pasta and alfredo sauce. Put the shrimp on top and sprinkle with parsley, and serve.

2.10 Baked Swordfish

Preparation Time: 5 minutes

Cooking Time: 22 minutes

Serving: 1

Ingredients:

- ½ pound of swordfish steak
- 2 tbsp. Of olive oil
- 1 tsp. Of garlic powder
- 2 lemons
- Sea salt, to taste
- 2-4 chopped green onions
- 2-4 tbsp. Of white wine
- Lemon slices, to garnish

Instructions:

1. Preheat stove at 375 degrees F (190.6 degrees C).

2. Utilize a profound, heating dish sufficiently huge to hold the swordfish steak.

First for the Marinade:

3.	On the lower part of the heating dish, add a tablespoon of olive oil, and one entire lemon, sprinkle with half teaspoon of ground garlic powder.

4.	Place swordfish steak on top of the main layer of marinade.

5.	Sprinkle on top of the swordfish steak with some additional virgin olive oil, the leftover garlic powder and lemon.

6.	Sprinkle some ocean salt on top of the steak. Add green onions. Put white wine on top, and let it sit for fifteen minutes to marinate.

7.	Bake for eighteen to twenty two minutes, or until swordfish is white or completely cooked.

8.	Add lemon sauce over the swordfish steak and serve.

2.11 Mussels with Tomatoes and Garlic

Preparation Time: 10 minutes

Cooking Time: 20 minutes

Serving: 4

Ingredients:

- 2 tbsp. of butter
- 1 chopped onion
- 3 minced cloves garlic
- 1 can of diced tomatoes
- 1/2 cup white wine
- 2 tbsp. Of chopped parsley
- Kosher salt, to taste
- Black pepper, to taste
- 2 lb. Of mussels
- Grilled bread, to serve
- 1 tsp. Kosher salt

Instructions:

1. In a pot over medium-low heat, warm the butter. Add onion and cook for five minutes. Add garlic and cook until fragrant.

2. Add diced tomatoes, wine, and parsley—season with salt and pepper.

3. Add mussels and stew until all shells are open.

4. Top with more parsley and present with barbecued bread.

2.12 Easy Shrimp Fajitas

Preparation Time: 5 minutes

Cooking Time: 12 minutes

Serving: 4

Ingredients:

- 1 tbsp. Of vegetable oil
- 2 cups of sliced red bell peppers yellow, orange, and red
- 1 thinly sliced onion
- 2 tsp. chili powder
- 1/2 tsp. ground cumin
- 1/4 tsp. garlic powder
- 1/4 tsp. onion powder
- 1/2 tsp. smoked paprika
- 2 tbsp. chopped cilantro
- 1 pound of large shrimp
- Lime wedges, to serve
- 4 tortillas
- Fajita toppings
- Pepper, to taste
- Salt, to taste

Instructions:

1. Heat the oil in a large pan over high heat.
2. Add the onion and peppers.
3. Season the vegetables with salt and pepper.
4. In a small bowl, mix stew powder, cumin, garlic powder, onion powder, smoked paprika, and salt and pepper to taste.
5. Add the shrimp and sprinkle the flavoring mix over the shrimp and vegetables.
6. Cook until shrimp are pink and misty.
7. Add cilantro and serve. Add lime wedges.
8. Serve the flour tortillas.

2.13 BBQ Salmon and Brussels Bake

Preparation Time: 10 minutes

Cooking Time: 20 minutes

Serving: 8

Ingredients:

- 2 tbsp. Of brown sugar
- 1 tsp. Of garlic powder
- 1 tsp. of onion powder
- 3 1/2 pounds of salmon
- 1 tsp. Of smoked paprika

- · 1 1/4 lb. Of Brussels sprouts
- · Chives

Instructions:

1. Preheat broiler to 450°F. Line two sheets with foil.
2. Mix sugar, one teaspoon garlic powder, one teaspoon onion powder, one teaspoon smoked paprika, and two tablespoons olive oil.
3. Divide one-fourth pound of Brussels sprouts.
4. Put sprouts on one sheet and add one tablespoon olive oil, one-fourth teaspoon salt, and one-fourth teaspoon pepper.
5. Cook sprouts for five minutes. While sprouts broil, prepare salmon.
6. Cut one side of salmon into ten filets. Brush the flavor, rub all over the salmon, and sprinkle salmon with one teaspoon of salt.
7. Mix Brussels.
8. Add salmon to the stove and cook for fifteen minutes.
9. Serve salmon with Brussels sprouts. Add chives on top.

2.14 Shrimp Fried Rice

Preparation Time: 30 minutes

Cooking Time: 10 minutes

Serving: 4

Ingredients:

- 3 tbsp. soy sauce
- 1 tbsp. sesame oil
- 1/2 tsp. ginger powder
- 1/2 tsp. white pepper
- 2 tbsp. olive oil
- 1 pound shrimp
- Kosher salt, to taste
- Black pepper, to taste
- 2 minced cloves garlic
- 1 diced onion
- 2 grated carrots
- 1/2 cup of frozen corn
- 1/2 cup of frozen peas
- 3 cups of cooked rice
- 2 diced green onions

Instructions:

1. In a small bowl, whisk together soy sauce, sesame oil, ginger powder, and white pepper.

2. Add shrimp in oil, and cook, until pink, around two to three minutes; add pepper and salt to taste.

3. Add garlic and onion to the skillet, and cook for around three to four minutes.

4. Mix carrots, corn, and peas, and cook, for three to four minutes.

5. Mix rice, green onions, and soy sauce combination. Cook for two minutes. Mix in shrimp.

6. Serve.

2.15 Fish Stick Tacos

Preparation Time: 10 minutes

Cooking Time: 30 minutes

Serving: 4

Ingredients:

- For Fish Stick Tacos:
- 16 Fish Sticks
- 8 corn tortillas
- 1/2 tsp. of garlic powder
- 1/2 tsp. Of smoked paprika
- 1/2 tsp. of onion powder
- 1/2 tsp. of cumin
- 1/2 tsp. of kosher salt
- 1/4 tsp. of cayenne pepper
- Cooking spray
- For Taco Slaw:
- 2 cups of purple cabbage
- 2 cups of shredded carrots
- 1/4 cup of cilantro chopped
- 3 chopped green onions
- 1/4 cup of pickled jalapeños
- 2 tbsp. of Greek yogurt
- 2 tsp. Of pickled jalapeño
- 1 lime

- Sea salt, to taste
- Pepper, to taste

Instructions:

1. Preheat the oven to 450 degrees F.

2. Add sliced cabbage, carrots, salted jalapeños, cilantro, and green onions to a medium bowl.

3. In a small bowl, add Greek yogurt, salted jalapeño juice, and the juice of one lime.

4. Add salt and pepper to taste.

5. Put aside.

For Fish Sticks Tacos:

6. Add garlic powder, onion powder, smoked paprika, cumin, salt, and cayenne pepper into a small bowl. Mix well.

7. Spray oil on the baking dish, and put sixteen fish sticks on it.

8. Place it in 450 degrees preheated stove for eighteen minutes. Flip it carefully.

9. While the fish sticks are preparing, heat eight corn tortillas.

10. When the fish sticks are done, form every taco by putting two fish sticks on top of every tortilla and taco slaw on top.

11. Serve and enjoy!

2.16 Coconut Shrimp Curry

Preparation Time: 15 minutes

Cooking Time: 20 minutes

Serving: 4

Ingredients:

For Shrimp Marinade:

- 1 lb. of shrimp
- 2 tbsp. of lemon juice
- ¼ tsp. of salt
- ¼ tsp. of black pepper
- ¼ tsp. of cayenne pepper

For the sauce:

- 1 tbsp. Of coconut oil
- 1 chopped onion
- 3 minced cloves garlic
- 1 tbsp. Of ginger minced
- ½ tsp. of black pepper
- ½ tsp. of salt, to taste
- ½ tsp. of turmeric
- 1 tsp. Of curry powder
- 2 tsp. of ground coriander
- 14 ounces diced tomatoes

- 13 ounce coconut milk
- 1 tbsp. of cilantro, to garnish
- Cooked rice to serve

Instructions:

1. In a small bowl, add shrimp with the ingredients of marinade. Cover with cling wrap, then refrigerate for almost ten minutes.

2. Add the onion in oil, cook for two to three minutes until the onion mollifies and gets clear.

3. Mix the ginger, garlic, salt, pepper, coriander, curry powder, and turmeric.

4. Add tomatoes, coconut milk, mix, and heat to the point of boiling. Cook for around five minutes.

5. Add the shrimp with the gathered juices from the marinade and cook for two minutes.

6. Serve with hot rice.

2.17 Fish Packets with Caper Butter and Snap Peas

Preparation Time: 10 minutes

Cooking Time: 25 minutes

Serving: 2

Ingredients:

- · 3 tbsp. Of softened butter
- · 3 tbsp. Chopped capers
- · Kosher salt, to taste
- · 1 lb. Of peas
- · 1 thinly sliced lemon
- · 3 fillets halibut
- · Basil, to garnish

Instructions:

1. Mix capers, butter, and one-fourth teaspoon salt. Add lemon.

2. Top peas with fish filets. Sprinkle each filet with salt and speck with butter—overlap and crease foil edges to seal firmly.

3. Cook in a microwave while keeping it covered, on medium heat for twelve minutes. Serve with topping of basil.

2.18 Red Curry Shrimp and Noodles

Preparation Time: 20 minutes

Cooking Time: 16 minutes

Serving: 4

Ingredients:

- 3 tbsp. coconut oil
- 1/2 pound of raw shrimp
- ½ sliced sweet onion
- ½ sliced bell pepper, red
- 1/2 sliced bell pepper, orange
- 1/2 tsp. salt
- 1/2 tsp. pepper
- 2 minced garlic cloves
- 1/2 tsp. grated ginger
- 2 tbsp. red curry
- 1/3 cup of peas
- 1 can of coconut milk
- 1 can of coconut milk
- 6 ounces of rice noodles, cooked
- 3 tbsp. chopped cilantro
- 2 sliced green onions

Instructions:

1. Warm a huge skillet over medium heat and add two tablespoons of coconut oil. Include the shrimp and cook until hazy and pink on the two sides.

2. Sprinkle salt and pepper over it. Remove the shrimp and place it in a bowl.

3. Add the leftover coconut oil to the pot.

4. Add onion, pepper, and salt.

5. Cook for around five minutes.

6. Include the garlic, ginger, and curry glue. Cook for five minutes.

7. Put snap peas and coconut milk in it. Increase heat to the point of boiling, then lower it, cover and cook for five minutes.

8. Add shrimp and cilantro. Cook for five minutes.

9. To serve, place a small bunch of rice noodles in a bowl and cover with the shrimp curry.

10. Top with additional cilantro or green onions.

2.19 Salmon and Ginger Rice Bowl

Preparation Time: 10 minutes

Cooking Time: 30 minutes

Serving: 2

Ingredients:

- 1 cup of brown or white rice
- 2 tbsp. Of butter
- 3 salmon fillets
- 2 tsp. Of curry powder
- 1 tbsp. Of lemon juice
- 1/4 cup white wine
- 12 ounces broccoli florets
- ¼ cup sliced almonds
- 1 tbsp. Of minced ginger

Instructions:

1. Cook rice.
2. Spot four salmon filets in a heating dish.
3. In a small bowl, combine butter, curry powder, and salt.
4. Add white wine and lemon juice to the preparing dish. Cook in the microwave until salmon is cooked.

5. Blend broccoli florets, water, minced ginger, and salt together in a bowl.

6. Take the salmon out of the microwave when done. Add the broccoli; cook for almost four minutes.

7. Mix one-fourth cup cut almonds into the rice.

8. Serve rice with cooked salmon and broccoli.

2.20 Shrimp and Zucchini Scampi

Preparation Time: 20 minutes

Cooking Time: 20 minutes

Serving: 4

Ingredients:

- 2 tbsp. unsalted butter
- 1 pound of medium shrimp
- 3 minced cloves garlic
- 1/2 tsp. red pepper flakes
- 1/4 cup of chicken stock
- 1 lime
- Kosher salt, to taste
- Black pepper, to taste
- 1 1/2 pounds of zucchini
- 2 tbsp. Parmesan
- 2 tbsp. chopped parsley leaves

Instructions:

1. Heat butter in a skillet over medium-high flame. Add garlic, shrimp, and red pepper chips. Cook until pink, around two to three minutes.

2. Add chicken stock and lemon juice; season with salt and pepper to taste. Bring it to a boil; mix zucchini noodles, around one to two minutes.

3. Add parsley and Parmesan, and serve.

2.21 French-Inspired Tuna Nicoise

Preparation Time: 10 minutes

Cooking Time: 20 minutes

Serving: 2

Ingredients:

- 8 potatoes
- 4 ounces of green beans
- 2 tomatoes
- ½ cos lettuce
- 3 eggs
- 100g of black olives
- 8 to 10 ounces of chunk tuna

For Lemon Nicoise Dressing:

- 1 1/2 tbsp. of lemon juice
- 4 tbsp. olive oil
- 1 minced garlic clove
- 1/4 tsp. of salt
- 1 tsp. of Dijon mustard
- 1 black pepper Black mustard seeds, one teaspoon

Instructions:

1. Boil potatoes until delicate, set aside. Cut into equal parts.

2. Boil green beans until delicate or done as you would prefer.

3. Put cos leaves on a huge plate.

4. Mix all ingredients of Lemon Nicoise Dressing.

5. Dissipate and layer the ingredients around the plate.

6. Add eggs, olives, and lumps of fish.

7. Top with dressing and serve!

2.22 One Pan Mustard Glazed Salmon

Preparation Time: 15 minutes

Cooking Time: 15 minutes

Serving: 2

Ingredients:

- 1 thinly sliced lemon
- 1/2 lemon
- 1 ½ tbsp. grainy mustard
- 1/4 cup of chopped fresh dill
- Kosher salt, to taste
- 1 1/2 tbsp. dijon mustard
- Black pepper, to taste
- 1 2- a pound of filet steelhead
- 1 pounds of new potatoes
- 1 pound of asparagus

- 4 to 6 cloves of garlic peeled
- 2 tbsp. olive oil

Instructions:

1. Preheat the stove to 450° F.
2. Put lemon cuts on the dish.
3. In a small bowl, blend grainy mustard, lemon juice, and dijon mustard together.
4. Add pepper and salt, one teaspoon of the new dill.
5. Put salmon on dish and rub it with the mustard sauce—season with legitimate salt and dark pepper.
6. Meagerly cut the potatoes and place them in a bowl with the asparagus and crushed garlic cloves.
7. Shower with olive oil, season with pepper and salt.
8. Cook vegetables and salmon for fifteen to twenty minutes.
9. Present with mustard sauce, add more lemon wedges and serve.

2.23 Grilled Stuffed Rainbow Trout

Preparation Time: 20 minutes

Cooking Time: 20 minutes

Serving: 4

Ingredients:

- 1 halved lemon
- 5 tbsp. olive oil
- 12 chopped cloves garlic
- ¼ cup fresh thyme
- ¼ cup of fresh rosemary
- 1 tbsp. red pepper flakes
- 4 whole trout
- Pinch of salt and black pepper

Instructions:

1. Add lemon, olive oil, garlic, thyme, rosemary, and red pepper drops in a bowl.
2. Rub trout with salt and pepper. Add the lemon-spice blend in it, and place it in cooler for one hour.
3. Preheat a microwave on medium-high heat and softly oil the mesh.
4. Flame broiled trout for around four minutes for each side. Serve with lemon wedges.

2.24 Salmon and Beets with Yogurt Sauce over Watercress

Preparation Time: 10 minutes

Cooking Time: 20 minutes

Serving: 2

Ingredients:

- 1 1/4 lb. Of beets
- 1/2 cup plain yogurt
- 2 tbsp. Dill, chopped
- 1/2 tsp. Of lemon zest
- 1 tbsp. Of olive oil
- 1 tbsp. Of poppy seeds
- Kosher salt, to taste
- Black pepper, to taste
- 4 salmon fillets
- 1 tsp. Of ground coriander
- 1 bunch of watercress

Instructions:

1. Take water in a medium pan. Steam beets until delicate, for eighteen to twenty minutes.

2. In the meantime, whisk together yogurt, dill, lemon zing and juice, oil, and poppy seeds in a bowl—season with salt and pepper.

3. Preheat the grill. Cook on a rimmed heating sheet, five to six minutes.

4. Serve salmon, beets, and watercress.

5. Add yogurt sauce.

2.25 Lobster-Noodle Casserole

Preparation Time: 30 minutes

Cooking Time: 40 minutes

Serving: 8

Ingredients:

- 2 lobsters
- 2 tsp. lemon juice
- For the Cheese and Macaroni:
- 8 ounces of elbow macaroni
- 3 tbsp. Of butter
- 3 tbsp. flour
- 1 tsp. salt
- 1/8 tsp. pepper
- 1 1/2 cups of milk
- 1 cup cheddar cheese
- 1 tsp. dry mustard
- 1 1/2 cups of frozen peas
- Black pepper, to taste
- 2 tbsp. of melted butter

Instructions:

1. Heat three to four quarts of water to the point of boiling in a stockpot. Put lobsters into the water. Cover the dish.

2. Cook the lobsters for around eight minutes.

3. Break the shells and take out the meat.

4. Cleave the meat and put it in a bowl; add two teaspoons of lemon juice.

5. Preheat the stove to 400^0 F.

6. Cook the elbow macaroni in a huge pot of salted water.

7. Add flour in the butter.

8. Add one teaspoon of salt and pepper. Keep on cooking for two minutes.

9. Steadily add the milk. Keep on cooking until the sauce thickens and bubbles for one minute.

10. Spoon around half cup of the sauce over the lobster, blend tenderly.

11. Pour remaining sauce over the cooked and depleted macaroni; add the cheddar and mustard and mix.

12. Spoon the macaroni and lobster combination into the pre-arranged preparing dish; top with the lobster blend.

13. Add breadcrumbs with two tablespoons of butter. Sprinkle pieces over the meal.

14. Cover and prepare at 400 F for around twenty minutes.

15. Then, steam the peas as coordinated on the package and season with spread and salt and pepper.

16.   Spoon the steamed prepared peas around the edge of the goulash not long prior to serving.

2.26 Lobster Mac and Cheese Recipe

Preparation Time: 10 minutes

Cooking Time: 20 minutes

Serving: 2

Ingredients:

- 4 tbsp. butter
- 2 tbsp. flour
- 2 1/2 cups of water
- 4 cups of milk
- 1 pound of corkscrew pasta
- 3/4 tsp. salt
- 1/4 tsp. garlic powder
- 1/4 tsp. onion powder
- 1/2 tsp. smoked paprika
- 1/4 tsp. pepper
- 4 cups of cheddar cheese
- 1 cup mozzarella cheese
- 1 1/2 cups of cooked lobster to garnish
- 1/2 cup of panko breadcrumbs
- 2 tbsp. chives

· Cooking spray

Instructions:

1. Preheat the broiler to 350 degrees F. Coat a two to three quart preparing dish with a cooking spray.

2. Soften two tablespoons of the butter in a pot over medium heat. Add the flour, cook for around thirty seconds.

3. Add water and milk.

4. Mix in the pasta, salt, garlic powder, onion powder, smoked paprika, and pepper.

5. Cook for ten to twelve minutes.

6. Turn the heat to low, add cheeses.

7. Overlap in the lobster meat. Move the pasta combination to the pre-arranged heating dish.

8. Add two tablespoons of butter into the panko breadcrumbs.

9. Sprinkle the breadcrumbs. Cook for ten to fifteen minutes.

10. Sprinkle with chives and serve.

2.27 Lemon-Parmesan Angel Hair Pasta with Shrimp

Preparation Time: 30 minutes

Cooking Time: 10 minutes

Serving: 4

Ingredients:

- 1 1/4 lbs. of shrimp
- 12 ounces of pasta
- 3 tbsp. of olive oil
- 3 Tbsp. of unsalted butter
- Salt, to taste
- Black pepper, to taste
- 3 cloves garlic
- 1 1/2 tsp. of lemon zest
- 3 tbsp. of lemon juice
- 3 tbsp. of fresh basil, chopped
- 3 tbsp. fresh parsley, chopped
- 1/2 cup of Parmesan

Instructions:

1. Cook pasta in salted water.
2. In a skillet, heat butter and olive over medium-high heat. Add shrimp, pepper, salt, and sauté for two minutes and add garlic and sauté until

shrimp has cooked through, around two minutes longer.

3. Put pasta in shrimp alongside one-third cup saved pasta water, lemon, and lemon juice.

4. Add more water one tablespoon at once. Add two tablespoons of parsley and basil, sprinkle parmesan cheddar, and serve warm.

2.28 Sheet Pan Shrimp with Broccoli and Tomatoes

Preparation Time: 30 minutes

Cooking Time: 10 minutes

Serving: 4

Ingredients:

- 1 pound of extra shrimp
- 2 tbsp. of olive oil
- 3 minced garlic cloves
- 3/4 tsp. kosher salt
- 1/8 tsp. red pepper
- Black pepper, to taste
- Olive oil
- 12 ounces of broccoli
- 1 cup of grape tomatoes
- 1 tsp. of fresh oregano
- 2 tbsp. lemon juice

Instructions:

1. Preheat the stove to 400°F.

2. Spot shrimp in a medium bowl with two teaspoons olive oil, garlic, one-fourth teaspoon salt, and pepper.

3. Shower a huge sheet skillet with olive oil.

4. Place broccoli and tomatoes in the dish.

5. Add two tablespoons olive oil, half teaspoon salt, pepper, and oregano.

6. Spread out in an even layer. Broil for fifteen minutes.

7. Get the sheet dish out of the stove and add shrimp, setting them uniformly around the veggies. Broil for eight minutes.

8. Top everything with lemon juice and serve.

2.29 Garlic Butter Shrimp

Preparation Time: 10 minutes

Cooking Time: 10 minutes

Serving: 4

Ingredients:

- 8 tablespoons of unsalted butter
- 1 1/2 pounds of medium shrimp
- Kosher salt, to taste
- Black pepper, to taste
- 5 minced cloves garlic
- 1/4 cup of chicken stock
- 1 lemon
- 2 tbsp. parsley leaves

Instructions:

1. Add shrimp, salt and pepper, to taste in the oil. Cook for around two to three minutes.
2. Add garlic to the skillet, and cook while mixing continuously until fragrant.
3. Add chicken stock and lemon juice for around 1 to 2 minutes.
4. Add six tablespoons of butter.
5. Add shrimp.
6. Add parsley leaves, and serve.

2.30 Grilled Lobster Tails with Herb Garlic Butter

Preparation Time: 10 minutes

Cooking Time: 30 minutes

Serving: 2

Ingredients:

- 3 lobster tails
- Lemon wedges
- For the butter:
- 125g butter
- 1 crushed garlic clove
- Parsley leaves, to serve
- 1 tsp. of Dijon mustard
- 1 pinch of chilli powder
- 1 lemon

Instructions:

1. Use kitchen scissors to cut along the highest points of the lobster shells, flip the tails over and break the ribs of the shell.

2. Utilize your fingers to open the shell and slacken the meat keeping it joined at the base and haul it half out.

3. Cook the lobster tails for ten minutes. Put them on a plate.

4. Present with lemon wedges and parsley.

2.31 Salmon with Chickpeas and Spinach

Preparation Time: 5 minutes

Cooking Time: 18 minutes

Serving: 4

Ingredients:

- 4 Salmon Fillets
- 4 tbsp. olive oil
- ½ tsp. kosher salt
- 2 cans of chickpeas
- ¼ tbsp. Black peppers
- 3 cloves of garlic
- 5 ounces of spinach
- 1 tsp. paprika
- 2 tsp. balsamic vinegar

Instructions:

1. Season salmon with pepper and salt.

2. Cook salmon in olive oil for around six to nine minutes.

3. Drain chickpeas.

4. Take out the salmon fillets.

5. Add more olive oil in the pan.

6. Add paprika and garlic.

7. Add chickpeas, tomatoes, kosher salt, and black pepper. Cook for five minutes.

8. Add spinach. Cook for two minutes.

9. Add vinegar.

10.   Season with pepper and salt.

11.   Add salmon in the pan.

12.   Serve it with spinach and chickpeas.

Chapter 3: Healthy Fish and Seafood Snacks and Salads Recipes

Pescatarian seafood snacks and salads recipes are well known throughout the world. Everyone should include these yummy recipes in their Pescatarian diet plan. Here are some of these recipes given below:

3.1 Crab Cakes

Preparation Time: 10 minutes

Cooking Time: 30 minutes

Serving: 8

Ingredients:

- 1/3 cup of mayonnaise
- 1 beaten egg
- 2 tbsp. Of Dijon mustard
- 2 tsp. Of Worcestershire sauce
- 1/2 tsp. Of hot sauce
- Kosher salt, to taste
- Black pepper
- 1 lb. Of crabmeat
- 3/4 cup of breadcrumbs
- 2 tbsp. Chopped Parsley
- Canola oil, to fry
- Lemon wedges, to serve

- Tartar sauce, to serve

Instructions:

1. In a small bowl, whisk together egg, mayo, Dijon mustard, hot sauce, Worcestershire, and season with pepper and salt.

2. In a medium bowl, mix together crabmeat, panko, and parsley.

3. Make eight patties.

4. In a skillet over medium heat, cover the container with oil and heat until shining. Add crab cakes and cook for three to five minutes.

5. Present with lemon and tartar sauce.

3.2 Shrimp Ceviche

Preparation Time: 5 minutes

Cooking Time: 30 minutes

Serving: 6

Ingredients:

- 1/2 cup of thinly sliced red
- 1 jalapeno
- 2 pounds of cooked shrimp cooked
- 3/4 cup of diced cucumber
- 1 cup of diced Roma tomatoes
- 3/4 cup of chopped cilantro leaves
- 1 chopped avocado peeled
- 1/2 cup of lime juice
- 1/4 cup lemon juice
- Salt, to taste
- 1/3 cup orange juice
- Tortilla chips to serve

Instructions:

1.   Put the shrimp, jalapeno, red onion, cucumber, avocado, and cilantro in a bowl.

2. Pour the lime, lemon, and squeezed orange on the shrimp.

3. Add salt.

4. Refrigerate for up to eight hours. Serve with tortilla chips.

3.3 Salmon Patties

Preparation Time: 10 minutes

Cooking Time: 20 minutes

Serving: 5

Ingredients:

- 1 of diced can salmon
- 2 thinly sliced green onions
- 1 tbsp. Of fresh dill, chopped
- 1/2 cup of panko bread crumbs
- 1/4 cup of Mayonnaise
- 1 tbsp. lemon juice
- 1 tbsp. Of Dijon mustard
- 1 beaten egg
- kosher salt, to taste
- Black pepper, to taste
- 2 tbsp. Of olive oil,
- Baby spinach, to serve

Instructions:

1. In a bowl, add ingredients—season with salt and pepper and blend.

2. Structure into five equally measured patties. Cook patties in clusters until brilliant and fresh, three to four minutes for every side.

3. Serve over spinach with lemon wedges.

3.4: Crab Hush Puppies

Preparation Time: 20 minutes

Cooking Time: 12 minutes

Serving: 8

Ingredients:

- 1 cup of yellow cornmeal
- 1/2 cup of flour
- 1 tbsp. sugar
- 1/2 tsp. salt
- 1/2 tsp. Creole seasoning
- 1/2 tsp. onion powder
- 1/4 tsp. baking powder
- 1/4 tsp. baking soda
- 1/2 cup of finely diced bell pepper, red
- 3 diced, green onions
- 1 lightly beaten egg
- 1/4 cup of buttermilk
- 1/2 cup of beer
- 8 ounces of crab meat
- Vegetable oil, as required
- For Remoulade Sauce:
- 3/4 cup of mayonnaise
- 1 1/2 tbsp. Creole mustard

- 1 tsp. horseradish
- 2 sliced green onions
- 1 tbsp. fresh parsley, chopped
- 1 minced garlic clove

Instructions:

1. Start by making the Remoulade sauce.
2. Mix all ingredients in a bowl and refrigerate.
3. In a huge bowl, mix together cornmeal, flour, sugar, salt, Creole flavoring, onion powder, preparing powder, red pepper and green onions.
4. Add the egg, buttermilk, and brew and mix to blend.
5. Tenderly blend in crab meat. Let sit for ten minutes.
6. Heat oven to 360 degrees.
7. Working in bunches, fry for two to three minutes.
8. Keep warm in a 200 degrees broiler.
9. Present with sauce.

3.5 Baked Clams

Preparation Time: 30 minutes

Cooking Time: 20

Serving: 6-8

Ingredients:

- 10-12 chowder clams
- 3 tbsp. minced onion
- 1/2 cup of butter
- 2 tbsp. fresh parsley chopped
- 1 minced clove garlic
- 1 tbsp. lemon juice
- 1 cup of breadcrumbs
- 1tbsp. clam juice
- Pepper, to taste
- Salt, o taste of
- 1/4 cup of Parmesan cheese

Instructions:

1. Fill a huge pot with half cup of water. Heat water to the point of boiling. Add the shellfishes to the bubbling water.

2. Let the mollusks steam for roughly six to ten minutes until the shells open.

3. Take mollusks out of the pot.

4. Preheat broiler to 350°F. In a sauté dish, add the minced onion. Cook for two to three minutes.

5. Add garlic.

6. Cook the garlic, add the parsley, bread scraps, minced mollusks, lemon juice, and shellfish juice.

7. Lay shellfish shells on a dish. Scoop a little stuffing blend onto each shellfish shell.

8. Sprinkle with ground Parmesan.

9. Prepare at 350°F for around twenty to twenty-five minutes until Parmesan is daintily sautéed on top.

3.6 General Tso's Shrimp 'n Broccoli

Preparation Time: 20 minutes

Cooking Time: 20 minutes

Serving: 4

Ingredients:

- 4 20 20
- 1 grated clove garlic
- 3 tbsp. Of soy sauce
- 2 tbsp. Of white vinegar
- 2 tbsp. Of sugar
- 1/3 cup ketchup
- 1/2 tsp. Of dry mustard
- 1 head broccoli
- 1 lb. Of shrimp
- Black pepper, to taste
- Kosher salt, to taste
- 1/2 cup cornstarch
- Vegetable oil, to fry
- 1 tbsp. Of sesame seeds

Instructions:

1. Put together garlic, soy sauce, vinegar, sugar, ketchup, and mustard in a skillet. Heat to the point of boiling.

2. Steam broccoli in a pot.

3. In the meantime, in a medium blending bowl, season shrimp with salt and pepper.

4. Dig shrimp in cornstarch.

5. Preheat a huge skillet over medium-high heat with 1/2" of oil and cook.

6. Spoon sauce over shrimp and sautéed food until caramelized.

7. Serve on top of steamed broccoli and topped with sesame seeds.

3.7 Bang Bang Shrimp

Preparation Time: 10 minutes

Cooking Time: 10 minutes

Serving: 4

Ingredients:

· 1/2 cup of mayonnaise

· 1/4 cup of chili sauce, Thai sweet

· 1/4 tsp. Sriracha

· 1 pound of shrimp shelled

- 1/2 cup of buttermilk
- 3/4 cup of cornstarch
- Canola oil, to fry

Instructions:

1. In a small bowl, add the mayonnaise, Thai sweet stew sauce, and Sriracha and mix.
2. In another bowl, add the shrimp and buttermilk.
3. Coat the shrimp in cornstarch.
4. In a hefty lined dish, add two to three creeps of canola oil and heat to 375 degrees.
5. Fry the shrimp until daintily earthy colored, one to two minutes on each side.
6. Coat with sauce and serve.

3.8 Simple Ceviche Recipe

Preparation Time: 15 minutes

Cooking Time: 15 minutes

Serving: 8

Ingredients:

- 1 pound of cooked shrimp
- ¼ cup of lemon juice
- ¼ cup of fresh lime juice
- ½ cup of fresh orange juice
- 4 diced plum tomatoes seeds
- 2 minced jalapeno peppers
- 1 cup of diced jicama
- ½ cup of chopped cilantro
- ¼ cup of finely chopped red onion
- 1 diced avocado
- Black pepper, to taste
- Kosher salt, to taste

Instructions:

1. Cut out the shrimp into half inch pieces and move to a bowl.
2. Mix the lemon, lime, and squeezed orange to join.
3. Pour citrus juice over the shrimp.

4. Permit the shrimp to marinate for fifteen minutes.

5. Add the jalapeño, tomato, jicama (or apple), red onion, and cilantro to the shrimp.

6. Mix the ingredients and left to marinade for an extra ten minutes.

7. Add avocado and the remaining juices.

8. Add pepper and salt. Serve quickly with tortilla chips.

3.9 Smoked Salmon, Avocado, and Fennel Salad

Preparation Time: 15 minutes

Cooking Time: 15

Serving: 2

Ingredients:

- ⅓ cup of mayo
- 1 tbsp. Of olive oil
- 1/3 cup of sour cream
- 2 tbsp. Of lemon juice
- 1/3 cup of chopped fresh dill
- 1/4 tsp. Salt
- 2 minced garlic cloves
- Salad (2 servings)
- 1/4 tsp. Of cracked pepper
- 1 head of butter lettuce
- 1 Turkish sliced cucumber
- 1/2 thinly sliced fennel bulb
- 4 to 6 ounces of smoked salmon
- ⅛ cup of red onion, thinly sliced
- 2 tbsp. capers
- 1 sliced avocado
- Sunflower sprouts

Instructions:

1. Place ingredients for dressing in a bowl and race until smooth, and blend in dill.

2. Add fennel bulb, lettuce, cucumber, red onion, tricks, and smoked salmon in a major bowl.

3. You can either prepare avocado and fledglings now or separate the serving of mixed greens.

4. Add avocado, sprinkle with pepper and salt, and serve.

3.10 Cilantro-Lime Shrimp Salad

Preparation Time: 10 minutes

Cooking Time: 10 minutes

Serving: 2

Ingredients:

- 1/4 cup red onion
- 2 limes
- 1 tsp. Olive oil
- ¼ tsp. Of Black pepper
- 1/4 tsp. kosher salt
- 1 lb. jumbo cooked
- 1 tomato, diced
- 1 avocado, diced

- 1 jalapeno, diced
- 1 tbsp. chopped cilantro

Instructions:

1. Put the lime juice, red onion, olive oil, pepper, and salt in a small bowl. Allow them to marinate for five minutes.

2. In a bowl, join slashed avocado, shrimp, tomato, and jalapeño.

3. Add cilantro, pepper, and salt to taste.

3.11 Shrimp Salad

Preparation Time: 5 minutes

Cooking Time: 10 minutes

Serving: 2

Ingredients:

- 1 lb. of shrimp
- 1 tbsp. Of olive oil
- Black pepper
- Kosher salt
- 1/4 of chopped red onion
- 1 chopped stalk celery
- 2 tbsp. Of chopped dill
- Butterhead, to serve

FOR DRESSING

- 1 lemon
- 1/2 cup mayonnaise
- 1 tsp. Of dijon mustard

Instructions:

1. Preheat stove to 400°F. On a heating sheet, throw shrimp with oil and season with salt and pepper.
2. Prepare until shrimp are dark, five to seven minutes.

3. Add mayonnaise, zest, and juice of lemon, Dijon, pepper, and salt in a bowl. Add shrimp, celery, dill, and red onion to a bowl and throw until consolidated.

4. Serve on bread or over lettuce.

3.12 Smoked Salmon and Oatmeal Salad

Preparation Time: 15 minutes

Cooking Time: 20 minutes

Serving: 4

Ingredients:

- 4 onions
- 6 diced tomatoes
- 1 diced ripe avocado
- 2 red chilli
- 1 lime,
- 3 tbsp. of wood chips
- 600g salmon fillets
- 3 tsp. Of rapeseed oil
- 125g of oatmeal

Instructions:

1. To start with, make the salsa.

2. Finely slash the green highest points of the spring onions. Blend in tomatoes, the avocado, and half

bean stew, and lime zest. Season and put away to marinate.

3. Brush the salmon with the rapeseed oil and spot it on the rack.

4. Cook on a BBQ or on a hob for eight to ten minutes. Keep warm.

5. For the oats, heat the leftover rapeseed oil in a griddle and fry the whites of the spring onions for one to two minutes.

6. Add the oats and cook for three to four minutes. Mix in one hundred and fifty ml water and lime juice.

7. Cushion it up with a fork and add any leftover tomatoes.

8. Serve the salmon fillets, salsa and oats.

3.13 Pan Seared Scallops and Quinoa Salad

Preparation Time: 25 minutes

Cooking Time: 20 minutes

Serving: 2

Ingredients:

- 1 cup of white or red quinoa
- 1 1/2 cups of water
- Kosher salt, to taste
- 1 tbsp. Of olive oil
- 2-4 tbsp. Fresh basil
- Ground pepper, to taste
- 2 oranges
- 1 finely diced avocado
- 3 tbsp. fresh basil
- 2 tbsp. minced shallot
- 1 1/2 tsp. minced red jalapeño
- Kosher salt, to taste
- Black pepper, to taste
- 2 tbsp. olive oil
- 10-12 ounces of sea scallops

Instructions:

1. To make the quinoa, place the quinoa in a pan, wash with cold water.

2. Add half cup of water and salt and heat to the point of boiling around 15 minutes.

3. Cushion the quinoa with a fork.

4. Add olive oil and basil.

5. Season with pepper and salt.

6. Cut the oranges down the middle, cut them into slices.

7. Add avocado, shallot, jalapeño, basil, pepper, and salt.

8. In a fry pan, over medium-high heat, heat olive oil. Season the scallops with pepper and salt, and sauté until practically springy to the touch, around two minutes for each side.

9. Spread the quinoa on two plates. Top with the salsa and scallops and serve.

3.14 Shrimp and Avocado Taco Salad

Preparation Time: 20 minutes

Cooking Time: 15 minutes

Serving: 2

Ingredients:

- 2 tbsp. oil
- 1 lb. Of medium shrimp
- 1 head of chopped romaine lettuce
- 4 diced tomatoes
- ½ finely diced jalapeño
- ¼ finely diced red onion
- 2 tbsp. Minced fresh cilantro
- 1 large diced avocado
- ½ tsp. salt
- 2 tbsp. lime juice
- For Taco Seasoning
- ½ tsp. salt
- ½ tsp. black pepper
- 1 tsp. ground cumin
- 1 tsp. dried oregano
- ¼ tsp. garlic powder
- ½ tsp. chili powder

Instructions:

1. Add shrimp and season with the taco. Sauté the shrimp just until each piece has begun to become pink.

2. In a huge bowl, put lettuce, shrimp, tomatoes, jalapeño, red onion, cilantro, avocado, salt, and lime squeeze.

3. Present with tortilla strips, and serve.

3.15 Crab and Shrimp Salad with Mango

Preparation Time: 15 minutes

Cooking Time: 20 minutes

Serving: 4

Ingredients:

For Yuzu vinaigrette:
- 2 yuzus, shredded zest
- 1 1/2 tbsp. of yuzu juice
- 1/4 tsp. kosher salt
- 1/8 tsp. Of fresh black pepper
- 1/4 cup of fruity olive oil
- For Soy-ginger mayo:
- 1 tsp. fresh ginger
- 1/3 cup of mayonnaise
- 1 tsp. soy sauce
- 1 1/2 tbsp. yuzu juice

For Salad:
- 2 mangoes
- 1/2 pound of cooked crab
- 1/2 pound of tiny shrimp
- 5 ounces of baby arugula
- 4 lime leaves

Instructions:

1. Make the vinaigrette: In a medium bowl, put lemon zest.
2. Add salt and pepper.
3. Add olive oil.
4. In a small bowl, mix all mayo ingredients.
5. Cut mangoes.
6. In a medium bowl, mix crab and shrimp with two tablespoons of vinaigrette.
7. In another bowl, blend mangoes and arugula with the remaining vinaigrette.
8. Top with crab combination. Sprinkle with lime leaves.
9. Serve and enjoy.

3.16 Shoyu Ahi Poke Recipe

Preparation Time: 10 minutes

Cooking Time: 10 minutes

Serving: 4

Ingredients:

- 4 10 10
- 1 pound of ahi
- ¼ cup of green onions
- ¼ cup of sweet onion
- 2 tbsp. shoyu
- 1 tsp. Of sesame oil

Instructions:

1. Cut ahi into pieces.
2. Cut sweet and green onions.
3. Add ahi, green onion, sweet onion, shoyu, and sesame oil to a blending bowl.
4. Tenderly mix to consolidate.
5. Serve and enjoy.

Chapter 4: Healthy Fish and Seafood Soup Recipes

Pescatarian fish and seafood soup recipes provide plenty of health benefits. They keep you full and also fulfill your nutritional requirements. Try the following recipes at home:

4.1 Lobster Bisque

Preparation Time: 20 minutes

Cooking Time: 55 minutes

Serving: 3

Ingredients:

- For Bisque
- 2 tablespoons butter
- 3 lobster tails
- 1 tbsp. olive oil
- 1 finely chopped onion
- 2 finely chopped carrots
- 2 finely chopped stalks of celery
- 1 tsp. chopped thyme
- 1 tsp. chopped tarragon
- 1 tsp. bouillon powder, chicken
- 1/2 tsp. salt

- 1/4 tsp. fresh black pepper
- 1/2 tsp. cayenne pepper
- 4 minced cloves garlic
- 2 tbsp. tomato paste
- 3 tbsp. flour
- 1 1/4 cup of white wine
- 4 cups of lobster stock
- 3/4 - 1 cup of heavy cream
- For Garlic Butter Lobster Meat
- 2 tbsp. butter
- 2 minced cloves garlic
- Pepper, to taste
- Salt, to taste
- Pepper, to taste

Instructions:

1. Fill a huge pot with five cups of water. Mix in one tsp. sea salt and heat to the point of boiling.

2. Add the lobster tails, cover with top and let bubble for five minutes, or until radiant red.

3. Eliminate lobster tails.

4. Set aside the fluid stock. When the lobsters are cool somewhat, eliminate the meat from the shells, saving the meat and any fluid that emerges from the shells.

5. Cook to the point of boiling, diminish heat to low and cook for a further fifteen minutes.

6. While the stock is stewing, cut meat into pieces and refrigerate.

7. Heat oil and butter in a pot over medium heat.

8. Add carrots, onions, new spices, and celery. Cook until delicate, around five minutes.

9. Season with the bouillon powder, pepper, and salt.

10.　　　Mix in minced garlic and cook until fragrant, around one minute.

11.　　　Blend in tomato glue, cook briefly to cover vegetables. Sprinkle over the flour and cook for a further two minutes.

12.　　　Pour the wine and cook. Mix in lobster stock, lessen the heat and cook while mixing periodically until the fluid has thickened and flavors have mixed around thirty minutes.

13.　　　Remove the heat, transfer the mixture to a blender, and mix until smooth. Then again, purée with a blender until extremely smooth. Get back to medium-low heat and add cream.

14.　　　Dissolve the butter in a skillet over medium heat. Sauté garlic for around thirty seconds, until fragrant. Add lobster meat, season with salt, pepper, and cayenne to taste. Gently sauté for one minute.

15.　　　Blend three-fourth of the lobster meat into the bisque. Fill serving bowls.

16.　　　Top each bowl with lobster meat.

4.2 Italian Fish Stew

Preparation Time: 20 minutes

Cooking Time: 45 minutes

Serving: 4

Ingredients:

- 8 ounces of fresh sea bass fillets
- 6 ounces of medium shrimp
- ⅓ cup of chopped onion
- 2 sliced stalks celery
- ½ tsp. minced garlic
- 2 tsp. olive oil
- 1 cup of chicken broth
- ¼ cup of white wine
- 1 can of diced tomatoes
- 1 can of tomato sauce
- 1 tsp. Crushed dried oregano
- ¼ tsp. salt
- ⅛ tsp. Black pepper
- 1 tbsp. fresh parsley

Instructions:

1. Defrost fish and shrimp. Wash fish and shrimp; wipe off with paper towels.

2. Cut fish into one-inch pieces. Slice shrimp.

3. Cover and chill fish and shrimp until required.

4. In a huge pot, cook onion, garlic, and celery in hot oil. Add one cup of stock and wine. Cook for five minutes.

5. Add tomatoes, oregano, pepper, and salt, and pepper. Cook for five minutes.

6. Add fish and shrimp. Lower the heat. Cook for three to five minutes.

7. Sprinkle with parsley, and serve.

4.3 Asian Shrimp and Vegetable Soup

Preparation Time: 15 minutes
Cooking Time: 35 minutes
Serving: 4

Ingredients:

- 12 ounces of large shrimp
- 4 onions
- 2 tsp. canola oil
- 2 thinly sliced carrots
- 8 ounces of oyster mushrooms
- 1 tbsp. Of fresh ginger
- 2 minced cloves garlic
- 2 cans of chicken broth
- 2 cups of water
- 1 cup of sweet soybeans
- 1 tbsp. soy sauce
- ¼ tsp. red pepper
- 1 cup of peas
  - 1 Hot onion sauce
  - Feta cheese

Instructions:

1. Defrost frozen shrimp. Wash shrimp and wipe off with paper towels.

2. Cut green onions into one-inch-long pieces, keeping white parts separate from green tops.

3. In a nonstick pan, heat oil over medium flame. Add white pieces of carrots, green onions, and mushrooms; cook for about five minutes.

4. Add garlic.

5. Add water, chicken stock, soybeans, and soy sauce, crushed red pepper, and mushroom blend.

6. Wait for it to boil, lessen the heat. Cook for around five minutes.

7. Add shrimp and pea pods to the pan. Cook for two to three minutes or until shrimp are murky.

8. Put green onion beat in it not long prior to serving. Decorate with fragmented green onions.

4.4 Salmon Chowder

Preparation Time: 15 minutes

Cooking Time: 15 minutes

Serving: 4

Ingredients:

- 3 tbsp. butter
- ¾ cup of chopped onion
- ½ cup of chopped celery
- 1 tsp. garlic powder
- 2 cups of diced potatoes
- 2 diced carrots
- 2 cups of chicken broth
- 1 tsp. salt
- 1 tsp. black pepper
- 1 tsp. dill weed
- 2 cans of salmon
- 1 can of evaporated milk
- 1 can of creamed corn
- ½ pound of shredded Cheddar cheese

Instructions:

1. Heat butter in a pot over medium heat. Sauté onion, garlic powder, and celery.

2. Put dill potatoes, pepper, stock, carrots, salt, and pepper in it.

3. Heat to the point of boiling, then cook for twenty minutes.

4. Add salmon, vanished milk, corn, and cheddar. Cook until warmed through, and serve.

4.5 Seafood Cioppino

Preparation Time: 45 minutes

Cooking Time: 2 hrs. 15 mins

Serving: 4

Ingredients:

- ¼ cup of olive oil
- 1 chopped onion
- 4 minced cloves garlic
- One chopped bell pepper, green
- 1 chopped red chile pepper
- ½ cup of chopped parsley
- Pepper, to taste
- Salt, to taste
- 1 tsp. Dried oregano
- 1 tsp. dried thyme
- ½ cup of water
- 1 can of crushed tomatoes
- 2 tsp. dried basil
- 1 can of tomato sauce
- 1 pinch of paprika
- 1 pinch of cayenne pepper
- 25 shrimp
- 1 cup of white wine

- · 1 can of minced clams
- · 25 mussels
- · 10 ounces of scallops
- · 1 pound cubed cod fillets

Instructions:

1. Sauté the onion, pepper, garlic, pepper, and chile pepper in the oil.
2. Add parsley, pepper and salt, basil, thyme, oregano, tomatoes, water, pureed tomatoes, paprika, and cayenne pepper; squeeze from the shellfishes. Mix well, diminish heat, and cook for one to two hours.
3. Add wine.
4. Around ten minutes prior to serving, add mollusks, cod, prawns, mussels, and scallops.
5. Turn on the heat and mix.
6. Serve your tasty cioppino.

4.6 Wild Rice, Shrimp & Fennel Soup

Preparation Time: 30 minutes

Cooking Time: 40 minutes

Serving: 6

Ingredients:

- 1 pound shrimp
- 1 fennel bulb
- 1 tbsp. olive oil
- 1 tbsp. unsalted butter
- 1 cup of leeks
- 1 carrot
- ¾ cup of uncooked rice
- ¼ tsp. Salt
- ¼ tsp. ground pepper
- 2 cans of chicken broth
- 1 cup of water
- ¾ cup milk
- 2 tbsp. flour
- 2 tsp. fresh thyme
- 2 tbsp. dry sherry
- 1 sprig of thyme sprigs

Instructions:

1. Defrost frozen shrimp.

2. Heat butter and oil in a pot over medium heat.

3. Add the slashed fennel, carrot, and leeks; cook for around eight minutes or until delicate.

4. Mix in wild rice, pepper, and salt. Cook and add stock and water. Bring it to boil; diminish heat. Cover it and cook for forty five minutes.

5. Whisk together milk and flour in a small bowl. Whisk the milk blend into the soup alongside thyme. Cook and mix until the soup is thickened.

6. Mix the shrimp into the soup.

7. Cook for two to three minutes.

8. Add sherry.

9. Top with the fennel leaves and thyme twigs, and serve.

4.7 Seafood Stew

Preparation Time: 15 minutes

Cooking Time: 25 minutes

Serving: 4

Ingredients:

- 3 divided garlic cloves
- 2 tbsp. olive oil
- 1/2 cup of fennel
- 3/4 cup of onion
- 1 tsp. Of divided kosher salt
- 1/2 tsp. Of divided black pepper
- 1/2 pound of cleaned squid
- 1/2 tbsp. Of tomato paste
- 1/4 cup of celery
- 1 tsp. dried oregano
- 1 cup of white wine
- 1 15-ounce can of crushed tomatoes
- 3 bay leaves
- 1 bottle of clam juice
- 1/2 tsp. of red-pepper flakes
- 1 1/2 cups of seafood stock
- 1/2 stick of unsalted butter
- 3 tbsp. Of chopped parsley, divided

- 1/2 tsp. lemon zest
- 1 pound of littleneck clams
- 1/2 pound of shrimp
- 1 baguette
- 1 pound of mussels
- ½ pound of white fish

Instructions:

1. Add onion, celery, fennel, half tsp. salt, and one-fourth tsp. of pepper in the oil and cook for six to eight minutes.

2. Add red pepper flakes and garlic. Keep on cooking for one to two minutes.

3. Add oregano and tomato paste.

4. Add wine, raise heat to medium-high, and cook for five to seven minutes.

5. Add tomatoes with their juice, bay leaves, stock, and cleaned squid. Heat to the point of boiling, diminish to a stew, and cook, covered, for thirty minutes.

6. Mix in one-fourth teaspoon of each salt and pepper.

7. In the meantime, blend the butter, lemon zest, parsley, and salt together in a small bowl. Spread the seasoned butter on toasts.

8. When prepared to serve, add shellfishes; cook for almost three minutes. Mix in the mussels and shrimp.

9. It is ready. Cut into pieces; serve hot with the gremolata toasts and Taco Bell sauce.

10.   You can also garnish with onions, sour cream, or cilantro.

4.8 Brazilian Fish Stew

Preparation Time: 10 minutes

Cooking Time: 25 minutes

Serving: 4

Ingredients:

- For Fish:
- 1 pound of white fish
- ½ tsp. salt
- 1 lime
- For Stew/ Sauce:
- 2–3 tbsp. Olive or coconut oil
- 1 finely diced onion- finely diced
- 1/2 tsp. salt
- 1 cup diced carrot
- 1 diced bell pepper, red
- 4 chopped garlic cloves
- ½ finely diced jalapeno
- 1 tbsp. tomato paste
- 2 tsp. paprika
- 1 tsp. ground cumin
- 1 cup of chicken stock
- 1 1/2 cups of diced tomatoes
- 1 can of coconut milk

- Salt, to taste
- ½ cup of chopped scallions
- 1 lime

Instructions:

1. Add salt, lemon zest, and one tablespoon of lime juice in the fish.

2. In a huge sauté pan, heat the olive oil over medium heat. Add onion and salt, and sauté for two to three minutes.

3. Turn heat down to medium, add carrot, chime pepper, garlic, and jalapeno and cook for four to five additional minutes.

4. Add tomato paste, flavors, and stock. Blend and cook.

5. Add tomatoes.

6. Cook for five minutes.

7. Add the coconut milk and salt.

8. Settle the fish in the stew until it is cooked for around four to six minutes.

9. Add coconut stock over the fish and cook.

10. Add lime.

11. To serve, serve over rice, sprinkle with cilantro or scallions.

12. Shower with a little olive oil. Spot one tortilla on top of the sauce in the dish, and spread a portion of the cheddar sauce on top of the tortilla. Top with the leftover vegetable sauce from the bowl.

13.   Place the second tortilla on top, add cheddar sauce and blended cheddar.

14.   Heat the sauce and cheddar until it is dissolved.

15.   Add coriander, Serve with avocado and bean stew.

4.9 Clam Chowder

Preparation Time: 15 minutes

Cooking Time: 30 minutes

Serving: 6

Ingredients:

- 4 diced slices of bacon
- 2 tbsp. unsalted butter
- 2 minced cloves garlic
- 1 diced onion
- 1/2 tsp. dried thyme
- 3 tbsp. flour
- 1 cup of milk
- 1 cup of vegetable stock
- 2 cans of chopped clams
- 2 bay leaf
- 2 potatoes
- Kosher salt, to taste

- Black pepper, to taste
- 2 tbsp. chopped parsley leaves

Instructions:

1. Cook bacon until earthy colored and firm, around six to eight minutes.

2. Add butter, garlic and onion in a pot, and cook for around two to three minutes.

3. Mix in thyme.

4. Add flour, milk, vegetable stock, shellfish squeeze, and sound leaf, and cook, whisking continually until marginally thickened, around for one to two minutes. Put potatoes in it.

5. Cook around for twelve to fifteen minutes.

6. Mix in cream and shellfishes until warmed through.

7. Season with salt and pepper to taste.

8. Add bacon and parsley, and serve.

4.10 Crab-Okra Gumbo

Preparation Time: 15 minutes

Cooking Time: 1.30 hours

Serving: 8

Ingredients:

- 15 1.30 8
- 1 cup vegetable oil
- 1 pound diced fresh okra
- 4 tbsp. butter
- 1 cup flour
- 2 cups of yellow onion
- 1 1/2 cups of bell pepper, green
- 1/2 cup of diced celery
- 2 minced garlic cloves
- 1 can of diced tomatoes
- 4 cups of shrimp stock
- 3 bay leaves
- 1 tsp. salt
- 1 tsp. Cajun seasoning
- 1 tsp. hot sauce
- 1/2 tsp. dried thyme
- 1/2 tsp. white pepper

- 1 pound of lump crabmeat
- 2 tbsp. fresh parsley
- 1 pound of shrimp
- 1 pint of oysters

Instructions:

1. In a huge nonstick skillet, heat three tbsp. of vegetable oil over medium heat. Add okra and cook, blending every now and again for twenty-five to thirty minutes or until okra is soft.

2. Eliminate from heat and put away.

3. Heat vegetable oil in a pot.

4. Add flour and cook and mix for thirty minutes, or until a dull earthy colored tone.

5. Add onion, pepper, and celery. Cook, regularly mixing for eight minutes.

6. Add garlic and cook for two minutes.

7. Add tomatoes, stock, cove leaves, salt, Creole flavoring, hot sauce, thyme, white pepper, and okra.

8. Stew for forty five minutes.

9. Add crab meat and parsley.

10. Cook for three minutes.

11. Add shrimp and cook for almost two minutes.

12. Add shellfish and cook just until their edges begin to twist.

13.   Present with rice.

4.11 Crab Bisque

Preparation Time: 10 minutes

Cooking Time: 55 minutes

Serving: 4

Ingredients:

- 3 tbsp. Of butter
- 1 finely chopped medium onion
- 2 finely chopped stalks of celery
- Kosher salt, to taste
- Black pepper, to taste
- 1 tsp. Of seasoning, Old Bay
- 2 minced cloves garlic
- 2 tbsp. Of tomato paste
- 3 tbsp. Of flour
- 4 cup fish stock
- 1 cup of dry white wine
- 3 bay leaf
- 1/2 cup of heavy cream
- 1 pound crab meat
- Chopped parsley to garnish

Instructions:

1. Add celery and onion in the butter, and cook until delicate, around five minutes.

2. Season with salt, pepper, and Old Bay. Mix garlic and tomato glue.

3. Cook until garlic is fragrant and tomato glue coats vegetables, around two minutes.

4. Sprinkle over the flour.

5. Pour in fish stock and wine; mix bay leaf. Lessen heat and let stew until fluid is decreased and seasons merge for thirty minutes.

6. Eliminate bay leaf and puree soup with a blender on high until extremely smooth.

7. Get back to medium-low heat and mix cream and half of the crab meat.

8. Cook for around five minutes.

9. Split between bowls and add crab meat and parsley before serving.

4.12 Slow-Cooked Shrimp and Scallop Soup

Preparation Time: 5minutes

Cooking Time: 3.50 hours

Serving: 6

Ingredients:

- 28 ounce of crushed tomatoes
- 1 Tbsp. tomato paste
- 4 cups of vegetable broth
- 3 minced garlic cloves
- 1 pound of yellow potatoes
- 1/2 cup of white onion
- 1 tsp. dried thyme
- 1 tsp. dried basil
- 1 tsp. Dried oregano
- 1/2 tsp. celery salt
- 1/4 tsp. crushed flakes, red pepper
- 1/8 tsp. cayenne pepper
- Pepper and salt, to taste
- 2 pounds of seafood
- Chopped parsley

Instructions:

1. Add all ingredients aside from the fish into a cooker. Cover and cook on high for two to three

hours or low for four to six hours until potatoes are cooked.

2. Add defrosted fish.

3. Cook for an hour until the fish is completely cooked.

4. Do topping with parsley. Serve hot with hard bread.

4.13 Lemon Salmon Soup

Preparation Time: 10 minutes

Cooking Time: 12 minutes

Serving: 4

Ingredients:

- Olive oil
- 4 chopped green onions
- ½ chopped bell pepper, green
- 4 minced garlic cloves
- 1 ounce fresh chopped
- 5 cups of chicken broth
- 1 pound gold potatoes
- 1 thinly sliced carrot
- 1 tsp. Of dry oregano
- ¾ tsp. coriander
- ½ tsp. cumin
- Black pepper and Kosher salt

- 1 pound salmon fillet

  1 lemon

Instructions:

1. Heat two tbsp. Olive oil in a pot. Add green onions, chile pepper, and garlic and cook over medium heat. Cook for around three minutes. Add half of the dill, and mix for thirty seconds.

2. Add stock, potatoes, and carrots. Add flavors and season with pepper and salt. Cook for five to six minutes.

3. Season salmon with salt and add it to the pot of soup. Lower heat and cook for a couple of minutes until salmon is cooked through, around three to five minutes.

4. Mix in lemon juice, lemon zest, and remaining dill.

5. Move salmon soup to serving bowls. Serve with dry bread.

Conclusion

A Pescatarian diet normally incorporates vegetables, grains, fish and seafood yet, for the most part, it avoids meat and dairy. The Pescatarian diet is broadly acknowledged similar to a nutritious decision because of the known advantages of a vegan way of life, combined with lean white fish, high-protein, and omega-3 unsaturated fats found in slick fish, including salmon, herring, and mackerel. This way of eating has shown a decreased danger of creating conditions, for example, type 2 diabetes, hypertension, and stoutness, which are all dangerous factors for coronary illness. Likewise, a recent report showed that omega-3 unsaturated fats are related to a lower hazard of lethal respiratory failures.

As per the studies, a Pescatarian diet helps to attain lower blood cholesterol levels, circulatory strain, and a lower hazard of diabetes. It also helps to treat metabolic disorders. The recipes given in **Pescatarian Cookbook** will help you achieve your desired health benefits.

Printed in Great Britain
by Amazon

13739005R00078